Preferred Internal Landscape

I0223639

Preferred Internal Landscape

Emma Winsor Wood

ORNITHOPTER PRESS   CHEVY CHASE

First Edition

Published by Ornithopter Press
www.ornithopterpress.com

ISBN 978-1-942723-19-6

Library of Congress Control Number: 2025937744

Cover photograph:
Untitled, 2017
© Emma Winsor Wood

Design and composition by Mark Harris

for Conner, who brought us there

Contents

Pour vivre heureux, vivons cachés

—French proverb

*No ideas but
in the facts*

—William Carlos Williams

I.

Manifest Destiny

At first the room was empty.

At first there was no room, just the idea of one.

At first there were only trees and the animals that lived in them. At first there was only weather. Later, asphalt, fences, roofs. At first the room was far-

fetched then right

here. Perfect, then prefab. Blueprint, then footprint.

At first there was the form; later, the content.

At first no one lived here, then we did. At first there were two red curtains then six. Too much room then not quite enough.

At first the landscape seemed full of hope. Then despair.

At first the dogs stayed close. Later, they roamed.

The first time I slept alone in the room, I couldn't.

The first time I tried to make a fire, I failed.

The first time I hiked, I startled at every step. The second time, I brought a knife.

At first it was just us. Then there were marveling guests: *Look at all the space you have.*

Then the mailman knocked daily. Then the dogs barked and kept barking. Other dogs barked back. In the distance, the faint beeping

of a truck backing up.

Freedom of Speech

All I want to do is write confessional poems but the world's not going in that direction anymore.

I spoke to a man on the phone about my potential as a voice-over artist and he said I "had the pipes" but not the passion. Call back in a few months, he said.

I've got a nasally ladyvoice, quick as Microsoft's brown fox.

What? my husband always asks.

Nevermind, I say.

Nevermind?

I want to speak more than I want to be understood. I want to be understood more than I want to die.

Death is so quiet.

Knock it off with all that singing, the famous poet tells her husband, also a famous poet: The world's not going in that direction anymore.

The cemetery sprinklers are on despite the drought. Because that grass is people. That grass is DNA.

We're really tired of the click-shut-closed ending after the 20th century, the poet says.

Later, in the cemetery, I repeat this to my husband on the phone. But he doesn't hear me.

What? he asks.

Nevermind, I say.

I want to hear what you said, he says.

All I want to do is write love poems. But the world's not going in that direction anymore.

I tell my husband I want him to fuck me—but really I want us to fuck until we've both been fucked.

My voice is so loud. It "carries."

Shh, my conservative ex-boyfriend said whenever we argued about politics in bed. *Shh*, Mommy says at the Met, in the car, on the N train to 34th Street. *Shh*.

I want to be heard more than I want to be understood.

What? you ask.

Nevermind, I say.

Nevermind?

In the Book I'm Proofing

The man's wife said she wanted
a dog. When he brought one home,
she ignored it. Was it a metaphor?
he asks once
then never mentions the actual dog again.

•

A lot of *eros*,
no sex.

•

The author's wife, who has Alzheimer's,
eventually forgets who she is—
who is she?
Is she?

•

"familiar but newly estranged"

"a planet consisting entirely of white and dark daisies"

"grown monstrously present"

"observable facts"

"artifact of compensation"

•

The same name spelled five different ways.

Visibility

When I lived in California, every tree was outlined in black, the poet says.

Downshifting down the NARROW WINDING ROAD, I notice a landscape of spiderwebs on the actual landscape, glowing spectral, wet, in the fog.

I used to wonder what distinguished "mist" from "fog"; now I know it's a question of visibility.

I am invisible here, in the fog.

My husband, C, is writing about "becoming-secret." He doesn't know exactly what that means, but hopes to propose a way of being outside capitalism, now that "former modes of resistance have been subsumed into it."

After the reading, the poet calls the man she's seeing a "friend." I notice she wears a maroon band on her left hand, ring finger. She's childless, post-menopausal.

Did you say you have kids? she asks.

I reply as if I don't want them

but sometimes I place a hand on my stomach and imagine something growing inside. A secret.

Without contacts, I can't see farther than ten feet. (That's fog.) With them, I can see

what looks like lavender purpling a neighboring slope. (That's mist.)

We live in a small valley surrounded

by trees. Behind them, more trees.

Personal Poem

I want to write a series of poems called "political poem." On the surface, the poems would have nothing to do with politics.

It's an impossible undertaking.

For instance, just yesterday, running, I saw a hawk hover for an instant before

plunging into the ice plant that lines the space between

pavement and cliff. It flew away, a rat

in its talons. For instance, I'd always thought the ice plant—a "creeping,

mat-forming succulent" that blooms into a profusion of narrow, colorful petals—

was native decoration. Now I know it's South African, introduced to stabilize

the state's eroding banks and has since smothered the indigenous coastal plants,

which once held song birds—yes, song birds...!

For instance, I read on a nature blog that the ice plant produces fruit: the sour fig.

It can be consumed raw, dried, cooked, pickled, or preserved.

But, the blogger says, she has **never** eaten the fruit of the ice plant and does **not** plan on giving it to her kids so eat it *at your own risk.*

Driving home after my run, the road beneath nearly invisible inside

the fog, a person in a white truck (I assumed young, male, white) was riding

my tail, the glare of his headlights making it even harder

to see.

Fight or Flight

We got home after dark to a whisper of moths worshipping our compact fluorescents—*their moon*, I thought, as I'd been taught to think, around the same age I'd learned the moon wasn't

my personal stalker. But Google teaches me the "moon theory" is only one of many used to explain the moth's self-destructive attraction to light.

Another is that male moths believe the light's a female telegraphing luminescent sex pheromones; they "die attempting to mate with the flame."

Another is that they perceive the bulb not as the moon but the sun and being nocturnal, eventually land, wings spread, to sleep—perchance to dream...

Another is that, in times of danger, their urge to flee directs them up to the light—any light—rather than down, into the dark. Another is that

we don't know. C took off his shoe and whacked the moths that had landed on our front door, leaving a trail of sticky remnants.

The way cleared, we darted in.

At every window, two or three, resting on or flapping into the illuminated glass.

Maybe we need more curtains, I said. Then walked around the house, switching off all the lights.

Proof

I'd like to be a minimalist, but I'm not

is another prophecy I fulfill

by creating it. When C and I first met

(I'm one of those who mentions her lovers too much

is another), we debated the existence of the self: I believed, he

disagreed. So, I related to him what my parents had related to me whenever
reminded of my lust for accuracy:

> When E was a child, we worried she'd never speak.
> Then, one day, age 3, reading a book with the babysitter:
> Look at this little bear's feet, the sitter said, pointing to the picture.
> Those aren't feet, E snapped. Those are *paws*.

See? (I said to C.) That's me.

Ancient Greeks occasionally used the base of a ruined column as an anchor

when they had nothing else

to moor the boat, he replied, unfazed.

I: Yes, precisely—the base of a *column*.

And he: A *ruined* column.

[...] [1]

---

[1] The silence on this subject lasted a few weeks but ended before the wedding,
one clean February day, when I turned to him and said: Maybe there is no self,
but also maybe, for me, there is.

Labor

I want to write a film script but instead I write a poem in the form of a script.

Some days, I put "go outside" on my to-do list.

There's an algorithm that can "translate" images—turn a Monet into a Van Gogh, a horse into a zebra, summer into winter.

I've been working on a translation for two years but have spent very little of that time actually working on it; I always have other work I need to complete before I can work on the work I'd like to be working on.

The problem isn't my emails, F said: The problem is my work. What I really need to do is eliminate my work, so I can write emails all the time.

I have a watch that reminds me to breathe.

Does an algorithm know labor, effort?

I'm not rich (I tell myself) because I hate to be told what to do. I'm individualistic because I'm a product of Reagan-Bush-Trump. I'm unhappy because it's winter, and I don't own a solar simulator.

We're all waking up and waking up and waking up ad nauseam.

(Another poet once told me never to use "we" in a poem, a symptom of the loss of the collective, of collective loss.)

We're in bed. It's morning, vacation.

We're waking up anew. We're awake.

We reach for the script, forgetting there is none.

II.

First Reality

In an act of pity his hands
are trees she cannot see for the forest
for a moment she forgets the elegance
in her grasp
white paper napkins fluttering in the wind
on an egg-blue bright day, she
cannot remember the clarity of the weather,
a telegram yet to be sent,
unspoken sentences, irrigation canals, the sky's vacant corral
the color of a drowned seagull

•

it was yesterday, will
the minute carousel, a souvenir, suffice
camellias twice muted beneath clouds caught
in fog
his starched shirt, white as a blister
all winter

    •

She stood at the window. There was
the small silhouette of her petrified woe
&, beyond, the frayed snow stitching itself into the earth
whose turf

•

Passing into the wilderness of twisted trees
between piles of moss & scree, thrum
of freight trains slipping past
a crow extracting a raccoon
folded into the road
supple white line painted rouge
whiff of rue

•

left, left sadly, but
pines blink the same snow aground
the city's vast, lonesome, a lost diagram
drenched, she misread
the black lines of benches, sharp against the unplowed stones, stepped
downriver

•

from it. The pain is
well-thumbed
a diving petrel
rising, tiring
bug legs severed yet still
squirming, the keen edge of an unset bone, freakish
her face, dented, in a mirror

•

anywhere, the tears upon her hands
collapse into a vitreous mask
the color of rust on the blinds' tangled slats
that ruined glance
an artifact

•

the nightmare. He
stood by while she plucked the barbed wire harp
into song—

Repeat the starved whisper, char
the dry flowers piercing
the pasture. Now, again, but
Wilder

•

and pain, bent
her hands into claws
frantic against the ligatures
clasping her neck like wax encasing
the dimples of a drowned orphan celebrated
in death in photographs in plaster casts in drawing
rooms around Paris
no respite

•

as a clock runs down. Walked backwards,
to perish for that, ornamentation
antlers hanging from rafters
the virgin beside a gold placard
what rapture

•

All night the sound
a rake over gravel, its flatness
a new grave

her wordless cry, her heartbeat tightening
hammering away
at velvet

the prefix

•

and then a quiet, a dull
throb, stray flakes dissolving into water
collage of litter, untitled, a spiral in the failing wake
grainy hush of Sundays
wind chimes

•

Or and, and as
a muted whine, red silk in a wooden bell
a copper triangle stilled between
fingers, no pulse
quicklime dusts the ravine
rustle of crêpe de chine
behind a screen
scene

•

all the darkness is
light's residue
a dew that, settling, saturates
a ledge

•

III.

Object Relations

In the morning, I wake up a subordinate

subject. I get out of bed and scrub my teeth the way Cinderella scrubs
the kitchen floor, oblivious to

the narrative framework. The existing power structures pick out

my clothes: long skirt, blue bra, sheer tank.

When I walk my dog, I pick up her shit with a biodegradable bag,
carrying it until I reach a trash can.

I'm a US citizen. My arm moves when I will it.

Later, on the phone with my mother, I make truth-claims, I share
resonant particulars, I laugh.

In the morning, I wake up inside

a lyric. The sun is setting. I am feeling many universal things.

I boil water for tea on the edge of a cliff.

The aesthetic pleasure I derive from looking at the panoramic view is
ideological.

I take a photo and post it to Instagram. It is a photo of my preferred
internal landscape. It is a photo of a landscape.

Saw your Instagram, my mom texts. *Hope you aren't out there alone.*

Outage (Day 1)

A house without power can't do any of the things a house is supposed to—can't heat, can't flush, can't shower, can't freeze, can't light. A house without power is just a lot of surfaces—to sit on, to lie on, to stand on. A house without power is very quiet and very cold.

We need to leave the "house" to get to the university where we work. We drive to the left: road closed. We drive to the right: road closed. We drive straight up: another road closed. I consult the map on my phone. We backtrack. We turn down a road we've never driven.

C's driving; I'm navigating. At the fork, you'll turn left, I say.

But when we get there (as I know because I've been following the blue dot on my screen), it's not a fork, but a turn-off onto a two-way single-lane dirt road. To its left, a pole that says,

NOTICE

PRIVATE PROPERTY

NOTICE

TRESPASSERS WILL BE VIOLATED TO THE FULLEST EXTENT OF THE LAW

NOTICE

THIS IS NOT A THRUWAY TO HIGHWAY 1

When we finally get through to Highway 1 on the road that's not supposed to take us there, I turn back to my screen to find out when our outage will end.

Paradise

Not a place to inhabit
But one that inhabits

    •

Hard to get to
So not everyone can

    •

There is one island in Hawaii where the residents still live as they did in
the 1800s—no cars, no computers, no cash. It's owned by white men,
who dictate the rules that keep it that way.

    •

A bird, a fish, a town just south of Las Vegas. Las Vegas.

    •

Whatever you think it is it is
Wherever you thought it was it was

    •

Once named, it closes like a fist around another fist

    •

Notice: Private Property
Notice: No Trespassing
Notice: Trespassers will be violated to the fullest extent of the law

    •

: an enclosure

All Around, Just Not Right Here

I wanted to write a list poem comprised of stuff that is "all around, just not right here," but all I could think of was "God," and that was not

a poem, just a fact.

Facts can be *in* poems, but they can't *be* poems.

The fact of me is not a poem, even if my creator (my mom) might think so.

My mom doesn't have the patience for poetry, but she likes it.

I don't really have the patience for poetry either

so I write poems for impatient people—matter-of-fact, easy to read.

When I started writing, I wrote elaborately about god-knows-what (love, mostly).

Now I write plainly about writing, sometimes landscape (dear god, the California landscape!).

My favorite writers are prose writers. My favorite gods, the ancient ones, their soap-opera lives. My favorite animal, the dog (isn't it

obvious?). When I was little, I believed in God. Now I'm grown up.[2]

---

[2] Yesterday, I ran off-trail to get to another trail I could see from afar; it looked easy enough—run straight. But the closer I got, the harder it became to see the path, any path. Eventually, I turned back.

Monument That Never Was

At the Queen's Palace, there is one bedroom for receiving guests of honor and one for guests to receive Her Honor.

In another room, the guard sleeps sitting up, his body another barrier between a would-be assassin and the king.

In another, one can follow the troops' movements through the landscape.

In the entry hall, the stone steps of the grand staircase, worn smooth by small aristocratic feet, are now worn smoother by mine (size eight).

I grew up running away from my parents in places like these, among intentionally ruined ruins.

I grew up daydreaming myself into the tiny beds of up-to-date dead queens.

That old-palace-smell—a mixture of damp stone and sloughed skin.

I imagine visiting this palace with my grandmother in the year of our Lord 1999. I imagine that smell is her.

Any object worth having, she told me, is worth taking by force.

The Queen's Park is now a dog park, this year just one in a string of very modern years.

Elsewhere, the painted ceiling appears to open onto a blue sky with clouds.

Alien

Traveling changes some things but not others: I still yell at C, *Turn now! now! now!* while he drives, but we have sex much more, at least daily.

There're loads of swans in Ireland, but most of them have necks the color of snow

a dog's pissed on. Most poems won't tell you that. Most poems want you to see pristine swans and snow, to see nature

as inherently pure, like a virgin or, yes, a swan.

In Dublin, we saw a book made from the hides of 135 slaughtered calves. If you look close enough, you can still see the hair follicles.

I wonder if the monks who made the book ate those calves with mint jelly.

That's how I used to eat veal. When I ate veal.

In Galway, we stood in a church built where a prison once stood. Same stones, new building.

On our last day, we drove to a spot that was only a half hour out of our way but looked remote on the map.

It was. The two-way road was barely wide enough for one car. We passed sheep, cows, stone wall

after stone wall. Where the road ended, we stopped and stepped out.

The land was muddy, dotted with sheep shit. It

arrested me. When we had sex later that night at the hotel near the airport, I bled a little on the bed.

I wanted/didn't want to go home.

History

A cartoon man in a cartoon hat

•

Clothes left so long in the washing machine they have to be washed again

•

Though the perimeter remains the same, the sands on the beach are constantly shifting

•

A "social construct"
(I think)

At the very least
a made-up thing

A religion

•

What will never be

•

Bedtime stories
for monarchs

•

Where the trains come from

•

Where I come from

Where I'm going

•

Song that never ends

Outage (Day 3)

The generator does its job, its exhaust leaking into the house through the cracked window where the heavy-duty extension cord's been snaked in to power necessities: the fridge, a light, our computers.

At first, we read exhaustively, now—

The situation's distracting, I say, even though at any given second, the potential is the same: either the power will come on or it won't.

We flip the switches, so we'll know the exact moment

we're no longer in the dark.

The generator does its job noisily, a steady thrum audible throughout the house, an airplane hovering overhead.

Nothing in the fridge has gone bad, but it smells in there. I think maybe it always smells, but that the noise and light usually cancel it out. Like the senses can only absorb so much at once.

When I plug in the toaster (we are used to such daily luxuries), the generator begins to whine.

In the end, it isn't the lights we've left on, barely visible in the midday sun, that signal electricity's return, but the sounds: a shuddering hum as the heat forces its way into our room, the sharp beep of the fire alarm changing power sources.

The dogs jump up, alert, excited, as if they too have been awaiting this connection. Maybe they have.

I plug the fridge back into the wall and bask in its electric glow.

The landscape's far away and getting farther.

Landscape of Fear
an erasure

Nighttime   forest

        a freshly killed deer.   the only

sound, the moon

       The lion   its eyes, glowing in the scant

hidden

            turns

       several nights, this scene repeated   at different locations

      scientists,   motion-

sensitive cameras,   carcasses

     the moment they heard a human

                                the big cats

fled

    cascading effects of

       this phenomenon   of

predation

                shifts when humans

                               terror-

(car collisions, habitat loss)

       the most benign form of human disturbance, our sound,"

unequivocal.

reaction

whether   or whether

hatred of

The controls

"Instead of the mountain lion   it's a human

they kill more

what cascading

effects

Smith said.

we're trying to achieve coexistence

under very specific circumstances — with

IV.

Realistic Life

Strings of white Christmas lights
A figure in the window, blurred, braless

Why shouldn't I be—
My figure in the window

I dreamt I had
A daughter

A blur
I remember now

I miss her

                                        I brush away
                                        Another fly

                                        My husband
                                        His coffee-cake, half-eaten

                              A brown ring at the base of his mug
                              Tears a dollar bill to pieces

                                        Concentrating
                          This what we talk about when we talk about—

                                        Cuts in

The abstracted look on his face
When he writes

A penny for
That gathering

I am still learning
How to be

Interrupted
& shut the door most days

The cover of the book he's left on the marble table
Geography of Nowhere

Curls back to its spine
In the moisture

Brown moth trapped
In a small paper lantern

A velvet knocking

I lose my keys in this house
Sand collects on the bed

My husband picks burrs off the dogs
Off our socks, the bathmat

Blue paint edges the
Window in the bedroom

The shades go up
Go down

I sauté
We eat quietly

Piling dishes he'll do later
In the sink

A whole day
Like this

On the brink

He said   I said   He said
He moved into the sun to sneeze

I cleaned the windows
From the inside

Pausing for
The guttural hum

A helicopter
At this hour

The white dowel that twists
Open the white blinds

Is swinging
Back & forth

A cold current enters
I moved it didn't I

That dream again with my ex
I can't quite remember

I was half daughter
& loved him accordingly

Electronic wind chimes
Wake up, wake up

& the dogs
Ready for their routine

                                        The kettle doesn't hold
                                        Enough for us both

                                        In the morning
                                        I boil just enough

                                        For myself

                                        A stray grain burning
                                        Into ash

The other side of the fence is
Elsewhere   *Come back*

Wading into a low muddy stream
A fawn leapt onto the path

In front just like that
Froth on her mouth

Sun's out on a cold day
The park, bereft of/free of

& she & me alone in it

                                        Small between trees
                                             We run on

                                          Uneven ground
                                      Shrubs scrape my shins

                                     Torso bare in the heat
                                   Thud of planks, suspended

                                       My dog, unleashed
                                             Briefly

                                              Wild

I nearly stepped on a bird
It flew upward

White rustle
& away

Behind me
A pick-up truck brakes

With a scream
No

I did

                                        The grass in our yard
                                          So wet mornings

                                        It's as if it rained
                                          In the last dark

                                              Unreal

                                          An imposter
                                        It grows much faster

V.

Controlled Burn

Everything's green for a month, then the rain stops, and it's brown again.

If she ever read it, Helen Vendler, a famous poetry critic my mom reveres, would call my work "simple transcriptive dailiness."

Everyone's entitled to their opinion.

I grew up hearing my mom say she hated the "brown hills of California," so when she visited, I turned her toward the ocean.

C says he can't really think unless he's at a big desk.

For me, it's about field of view.

I want to see everything all at once.

Determinism

At the side of the road, a bloated deer, her legs still curled into canter.

On the tip of the branch, a web bloated with the larva of the fall webworm.

I get it now; it's only green in places where the rivers run year-round.

Evolutionary Process

The birds learned to imitate the payphone ringing

The waterfall created the wind

The trees grew out, not up

-

"There was no way to reroute what had already been routed"

-

Boy cones and girl cones

Long arms way up top

(for stability)

-

"What is the role of the poet

assumes there is a role"

-

A bear built his nest in a man's bedroom
while the man slept outside
between propane-fueled space heaters
by his horse's grave

-

"Typically, I take 10 to 20 years to write a poem"

•

Stranded in

The Nut

"It's hard to love someone people think is not worth loving anymore," the woman says to her friend at the café.

Later, they talk about dogs, how she likes to guess who the owner is when she sees one waiting outside. She guesses, guesses wrong.

I get up and go, they go on talking.

The sun is shining but not hot, not too hot.

This is rare. Something is usually always too something for me.

This is because I am very sensitive, which is another way of saying perpetually unsatisfied.

It is difficult to find the right balance, any balance.

Good writing is not balanced but life is, good life, that is.

My life is good because it is increasingly balanced, or my life is good when it is balanced: both are true.

My balance has always been bad—that's why I couldn't ride a bike till I was 12, that's why I was always falling off horses.

I am easily shaken, shaken off.

"His poems were just random collections of facts about himself. They were bizarre," my adjunct friend says.

The sand in my pockets falls out of my pockets.

He is reading some of my poems now, I am guessing he doesn't like them.

I am learning about comma splices and misplaced modifiers so I can teach my students how to avoid them.

I myself learned how to write correctly without learning any terms I can remember.

This means I'm lying to them, my students (that's an appositive), when I say it is "critical" they learn these terms themselves.

I meet a college student who speaks two languages and doesn't know what a subject is, a high school student who thinks a noun is an adjective.

They were just given language and told to use it.

I guess a mechanic given tools without being told how to use them might eventually figure it out, but she would probably end up using a

hammer to crack open a nut. It works, but it smashes the nut.

Free Will

My car pulls to the right.

The man who tried to align my tires tells me I've got to choose: either the tires or the steering.

If the steering's perfect, he explains, the tires will wear out fast. (How fast? I ask. *Fast*, he repeats). If the tires're perfect, the steering will drift. You'll have to, you know, *hold* the steering wheel, he says.

As a boy, C's left eye didn't want to work; it wandered. He had to wear glasses for years to fix it. Now it looks where it's told to look, unassisted.

Most people, the man says, would choose the tires.

My eyes don't wander but they are "impaired." Every day, I put on my glasses and objects become distinct from each other, separate. I'm told this is what it means to see.

The other day, I overheard a woman say she asked her doctor if there were exercises she could do to improve her eyesight. There were, he answered...

I didn't hear the rest.

The man at the auto shop is waiting for my answer. I choose the tires, too, I say, pulling out my wallet.

Judgment Call

In the book I'm reading, a woman wakes up every morning and asks herself:

What will I do to make myself happy today?

I decide to stop reading the book.

Perspective

Photos of a successful young poet

appear in my feed. For an instant,

I feel a familiar heat rising—

then I recall that

for a long time,

he was dying

and now

he's dead.

Rabbit Test

It was so tiring to be that age, just waiting,

N says over the speakers in the dimly-lit hangar that used to be filled with ice in the winter.

I nod though I miss that feeling and mourned it when I married, another milestone in the rearview.

Is that what I want

when I say I want to return

to high school—to be tired, waiting?

Later, back in the room I grew up in, I call C:

I felt ambivalent when I graduated, I say, yet now I feel high school was one of the happiest times of my life.

Nostalgia comes from misremembering, he says.

When he was just out of high school, my grandfather wrote a story called "A Very Young Rabbit."

There's no actual rabbit in the story—just a girl, based on his little sister.

She died after him, having lost the names of all eight of her children.

I was given her name.

In the 1950s, the most common way to determine whether you were pregnant was the rabbit test:

a doctor would collect your urine, inject it into a live female rabbit, then cut her

open. If you were pregnant, her ovaries would show "follicular maturation."

If not, her ovaries showed nothing, and now she was dead.

It reminds me of the old test for witches: tie the woman up—if she floats, she's
a witch. Of course, they all sank. Dead women, dead rabbits, dead

champagne in the dimly-lit hangar where N's still speaking to me, asking how
California's changed

my poems, raising his eyebrows in what can only be disapproval when I say I've
written an entire manuscript in the span of a few months,

and I am thinking of the ice melting in my vodka soda on the table a few feet
away, not about poetry, as I tell him

that last spring, the dogs dug out a burrow in our backyard

exposing four young rabbits, which barely filled my palm

when I picked them up, in leather garden gloves, to move them

though I knew moving them

would kill them

as surely as leaving them there—

To my right, the girl I made out with once in college is hitting on a boy she
never talked to in high school; to my left, the first boy I kissed, dumped, and
later loved

is swaying drunkenly beneath a cowboy hat, and N is waiting

for me to go on, but I have made my point

I think.

Living

It's hard for me to distinguish between my writing life and my life, C says.

I write this down in my phone beside notes about elephant seals.

"It's best they don't even know we've been here," our guide said.

And, "I know it's tempting but don't wave at the seal pups."

A few minutes later, I involuntarily waved at a pup. She was staring at me, tilting her head

the way my dog does when I play videos of babies crying—videos I play only so I can watch

my dog do this. The baby videos I prefer to watch are of deaf babies who have been given hearing aids. When they hear their mother's voice for the first time, they widen their eyes

and smile silently. Half the seal pups will die in their first year of life.

At the turn of the last century, scientists believed elephant seals had gone extinct.

They hadn't. Turned out they were just lying low in Guadeloupe.

When scientists discovered this, they killed seven of the nine they found. To bring home. For proof.

On the tour, we also saw a harbor seal; our guide said he "wasn't going to make it." He was skinny.

He was starving.

"His death is natural. We don't like to interfere with nature," our guide said calmly, smiling.

There's an island a mile or so off the coast where the lighthouse keeper and his family used to live.

When the lighthouse was replaced with a buoy, the structures were abandoned. Now, the seals live there.

Three cameras observe the island night and day, livestreaming the seals' lives.

The island is entirely bare and brown. The seals killed all the vegetation when they took over.

Fake News

TV SHOW CONTESTANTS SPEND YEAR IN WILDERNESS – WITH NO ONE WATCHING, the headline reads.

Elsewhere, I read about a start-up that's trying to bring three species back from extinction. This is called "de-extinction."

In Stockholm, most of the churches are situated in the center of a large square of grass, dissected by a series of diagonal paths.

The first time we walked through one, I thought it was a garden. Then I realized it was a cemetery.

A garden is 1) a plot of land used for growing flowers or fruit or vegetables; 2) ground set aside for public recreation.

A cemetery is a plot of land set aside for the burial of human bodies and their remains.

There are often flowers in a cemetery, but they have usually been grown elsewhere.

Flowers get taken to cemeteries for the same reason people get taken to hospitals—to die.

One conservationist said, of de-extinction, It would be one step forward, and three to eight steps back.

I take four steps back (to get a picture of the church) and trip on a footstone.

In England, footstones were used to indicate the deceased was a murderer.

In the US, they are used to indicate that the deceased served in the Armed Forces.

At one English cemetery, the preponderance of footstones indicates many murderers must have been buried there—but who or why, we don't know:

soldiers used the cemetery records as kindling during World War II.

In the US, many laid-off blue-collar workers, mostly men, are looking for the jobs they used to have, even though those jobs have left the country for good.

One economist calls this "retrospective wait unemployment."

The TV network that kept filming the contestants even after the show had been cancelled reasoned it might still be watched,

retrospectively. They are simply waiting for the right time to air it.

The air has turned all the grave angels the color of frozen grass.

By now, my fingers have lost all feeling. I reach through the neckline of my sweater and press them into the slightly sticky space under my arms.

No one's watching.

Soon we'll be home. In the wilderness.

Notes

"Manifest Destiny": This poem is written after Elizabeth Willis's poem "Plot."

"In the Book I'm Proofing": The text in quotes originally appeared in *Eros and Illness* by David B. Morris (Harvard University Press, 2017).

"Fight or Flight": This poem includes a quote from "Notes from the Lab: Like a Moth to a Flame" by Brenna Shea, published July 22, 2021 on the Missoula Butterfly House and Insectarium website.

"First Reality": Each poem in this sequence begins with a first line borrowed from a poem by Robert Creeley.

"Landscape of Fear": This poem is an erasure of Sarah Kaplan's article "Mountain Lions are Terrified by the Voices of Rush Limbaugh and Rachel Maddow," published in *The Washington Post* on June 21, 2017.

"Controlled Burn": The words "simple transcriptive dailiness" come from "Words That Sing, Dance, Kiss," a review Helen Vendler published in *Poetry* in May 2017.

"Fake News": The poem's opening headline is the title of an article by Hannah Ellis-Petersen that appeared in *The Guardian* on March 23, 2017.

Acknowledgments

I am grateful to the editors who saw something in these poems and published versions of them in their journals: thank you to *Bear Review, Bennington Review, BOAAT, Columbia Review, DIAGRAM, The Fourth River, jubilat, Jung Journal, The Maynard, Meridian, New Delta Review, Pouch, Prelude, Seattle Review,* and *ZYZZYVA.*

Thank you to the many editors at small presses who saw something in this manuscript as I submitted versions of this book over the years: Autumn House Press, BOAAT Books, Burnside Review, The Center for Literary Publishing at Colorado State University, CSU Poetry Center, Fence, Fonograf Editions, Mad Creek Books, Noemi Press, Switchback Books, the University of Wisconsin Press, and Zone 3 Press.

Thank you to the teachers who helped guide these poems—Jim Galvin, Forrest Gander, Brenda Hillman, Mark Levine, Sharon Olds, Brenda Shaughnessy, and Elizabeth Willis—as well as to the support of the Community of Writers and the Napa Valley Writers' Conference where some of these poems began.

I'd like to thank friends, mentors, and acquaintances who read and encouraged me and/or this work, and especially to those who extended friendship during our early days in Santa Cruz: Aamina Ahmad, Kris Bartkus, Emily Bark Brown, Lily Brown, Charlotte Bruce-Byrne, Louise Bruce, Emmett Buckley, Chris Chen, Ross and Kelsey Clifford, Brian Cochran, Darcie Dennigan, Elisa Gabbert, Will Jameson, Sophia Dahlin, Tye Kindinger, Jami Macarty, Louise Marburg, Patty Nash, Katie O'Hare, LuLing Osofsky, Micah Perks, Caitlin Roach, Claude Rosen, Joe Sherlock, Kelsi Vanada, Kirstin Wagner, Ronaldo Wilson, James Yu, and Danielle Zaychik.

Thanks to Danielle Cote, Karrie Gaylord, Nicole Schowalter, and to the members of Arete Women's Running Club from 2018-21, all of whom helped me enter the Santa Cruz landscape, with company—and to my dogs, Franny and Charlie, for the same.

Many of these poems started in a shared document with Kelsi and Kris—thank you!

Thanks finally, to my parents, Clem and Sally Wood.

And to Conner, for everything else.

About the Author

Emma Winsor Wood is the author of *The Real World* (BlazeVOX, 2022) and the translator of *A Failed Performance: Short Plays and Scenes of Daniil Kharms* (Plays Inverse, 2018). She currently teaches at Xavier University in Cincinnati, Ohio.

www.ingramcontent.com/pod-product-compliance
Lightning Source LLC
Chambersburg PA
CBHW022205080426
42734CB00006B/564